ABOUT THE AUTHOR

James A Ward is a published author, having written for children, teenagers and adults. He has also written comedy for TV and radio, both in the UK and mainland Europe.

As well as scripting gags and sketches for, among others, Freddie Starr, Roy Hudd and June Whitfield, his work has been broadcast on Radio 2, Radio 4, the World Service, BBC1, ITV and S4C (Wales). He has also performed stand-up comedy across Yorkshire and at the Edinburgh Fringe.

A member of The Magic Circle and the Harrogate Society of Magicians, James has lectured and performed around the UK and as far away as India. He has performed mindreading magic on TV and radio, and created almost a hundred original tricks which have been published in magazines and e-books around the world.

An after-dinner speaker, his range of topics includes his misadventures as both a former criminal lawyer and a magician, the life and times of the great English character actress, Margaret Rutherford, and the exciting world of memory techniques. He also holds a performance qualification from the London Academy of Music and Dramatic Art – and an ice-skating certificate for, at the age of 12, having travelled ten yards in a straight line without falling over.

In his spare time, he writes comedy and crime books.

www.jamesward.co.uk

Other books by James A Ward

(Available via Amazon and/or www.lulupublishing.com)

Writing as Bernard Fling

X Marks the Spot

Bernard to the Rescue!

Writing as James Alexander

Wait to Deceive

When the Devil Calls

SLEIGHTLY AMUSING

James A Ward

To Mike Coyne

30 April 1939 – 3 September 2014

A gifted comedian, magician and dear friend

CONTENTS

INTRODUCTION

Though this book is aimed primarily at magicians, most if not all of the jokes included can easily be rewritten to accommodate other performance situations. (Just substitute your own occupation for 'magician', and the job is often done.)

Humour is inherently subjective. What makes one person laugh may leave another cold. Jokes are also endlessly recyclable – which is both a blessing and a curse. On the one hand, it means you can often take an existing joke and rewrite it for a different situation or personality – sometimes many years apart. (Jokes based on people's size, looks and perceived intellectual shortcomings are common examples.) On the other hand, it means it's easy to reinvent the wheel – and create what you imagine to be an original joke, only to discover it's been done before. I have aimed to create original material in this book but if, at any point, you have a sneaking suspicion you've seen something similar in the past – forgive me. It's entirely unintentional, but, with joke writing, an almost inescapable hazard. (I know – I've been on the receiving end, innocently enough, several times over the years.)

The book is divided into two sections, the first of which is an exploration of the comedy-writing process. This involves a brief foray into the theory behind what makes us laugh, followed by an outline of basic joke-writing techniques which should enable you to sit down and, hopefully, create your own material. It is not my intention to produce an exhaustive text on comedy writing and, to that end, I conclude with a bibliography of books to take your own joke-writing further should you feel suitably inspired.

Which I hope you will!

The second half of the book comprises more than 400 jokes, bits of business (not all my own) and patter. I hope you'll find something useful there. Though many of the jokes would suit a broad range of situations, a number have been written with magicians and magical comperes in mind. I hope most of them will make you laugh, though – inevitably – I'm sure a few will make you groan!

Hopefully, several will leave you thinking, 'I can do better than that!' In which case, I wish you luck.

Whatever you take out of this book – have fun! It is, after all, what humour is all about.

COMEDY WRITING FOR BEGINNERS

INTRODUCTION

In the following pages, I want to examine – briefly – the nature of comedy and why we laugh. We'll then go on to examine a few gag-writing formulae, and look at how to construct your own material.

1. Why do we laugh?

We laugh for a variety of reasons, and I won't attempt to list them all here. For current purposes – and with magic in mind – I'll restrict myself to the following:

  (a) Surprise

  (b) Incongruity

  (c) Release

Surprise

Magic and comedy have much in common. In both, our aim is to misdirect.

'I'm going to turn this card into another one – look, I've done it' – is in no way magical, however skilful the transformation, because you telegraphed the conclusion. It would be like giving the punch line of the joke, followed by the set-up.

We laugh when we're surprised – when something pulls us up short, when it's unexpected.

A classic visual joke with which we're all familiar is the venerable 'slipping on a banana peel' gag. A screenwriter once asked Charlie Chaplin for advice on how to freshen it up, convinced it had been done to death and would no longer raise a laugh. Should he first show the peel, he asked Chaplin, then the victim (in this case a fat lady), then the fall? Or should he show the fat lady first, then the peel on which she slips? Chaplin replied: 'You show the fat lady approaching; then you show the banana peel; then you show the fat lady and the banana peel together; then she steps over the banana peel *and disappears down a manhole.*' By derailing expectations – and surprising the viewer – Chaplin breathed new life into an old joke.

In verbal humour, we laugh because the punch line is unexpected. Examine your favourite gags and you'll see that those you enjoy the most are those in which the final line catches you by surprise. A telegraphed joke may still make us smile, but the one we prefer is the one that hits us over the head while we're not looking.

Incongruity

We laugh when something is out of place, or not as it should be. This humour is often visual. Magical sight gags include expanding props such as ladders and the like that emerge from small containers. Another old favourite is the 'long card', where the magician starts to remove a playing card from his jacket – say the two of hearts. He continues pulling it out to reveal it's not an ordinary card at all – it's a very long card: anything from the two up to the ten and maybe even beyond. We laugh because reality has been distorted.

Or, as the Canadian humorist Stephen Laycock once wrote:

'Humour results from the contrast between a thing *as it is and ought to be*, and a thing smashed out of shape, *as it ought not to be.*'

If you hand a helper a pack of A4-sized cards and ask her to shuffle, or offer miniature cards to a well-built, strapping young man for the same purpose, in all likelihood people will laugh – because the sight alone is not what they expect. The situation is *not as it is and ought to be*. It is *as it ought not to be* – ie it's incongruous – and we laugh.

Release

We laugh when there's been a build-up of tension and that tension is released. We will all, at some time or another, have heard what purports to be a serious story. When, in the final sentence, the joke is sprung on us we laugh – partly from surprise, perhaps, but also because laughter is a form of relaxation – and we are relieved because the tension has been lifted.

The comedy magician, Tommy Cooper, was a master of this type of humour. Time and again, he would suggest a trick was about to go disastrously wrong. He would look concerned and that concern – albeit tinged with humour – would convey itself to us. At the very last, when the trick worked, Tommy would look relieved and chuckle like a mischievous child. Relieved, also, we would laugh along with him.

To sum up, when constructing humour – whether verbal or visual – ask yourself:

- How can I surprise people by leading them in one direction before taking them somewhere else?
- How can I distort or change something so that it's not what people would normally expect it to be?
- How can I build up the tension before releasing it?

Combine all three into a single routine and you're on your way to comic success.

2. Character

Though perhaps more important for a stage performer, even a table-hopper should have an easily identifiable, and predominant, trait.

There are many possible characters: 'Jolly', 'Camp', 'Nervous', 'Aggressive' and so on. You may wish to adopt a very different persona to your own, or exaggerate your own character a little. Or you may just want to be yourself.

To a large extent character will both create and drive your humour. By that, I mean humour should not only be consistent with character, but should arise out of character. The comedy mindreader Graham P Jolley, for example, has an aggressive approach. His humour is largely, if not exclusively, directed at his audience. Were he to launch into a humorous examination of his own faults, he would lose that consistency and we would be far less likely to laugh.

The American comedy magician, Mac King, by contrast, has a gentler, more friendly persona, which is reflected in his humour. Were he to fire a tirade of abuse at his helpers, we would regard this as out of character, with the result that we would feel uncomfortable and unsure – and the laughs would, in all likelihood, dry up altogether.

Your character will also define the type of humour you feel comfortable with. If you are sensitive, even a little unsure of yourself – whether because this is how you are, or how you wish to portray yourself – then you are unlikely to lean towards aggressive humour. You are more likely to favour self-deprecating remarks, or attack third parties whom your audience are also likely to find worthy targets.

So give some thought to who you are when you perform. Don't worry that this eliminates some great gags from your act; the best gags are the ones that suit you – not someone else.

3. Targets

All humour has a target, and your approach to comedy may be dictated by the target you select.   As a magician, you have three potential targets: (a) the audience, (b) yourself, (c) third parties (ie absent targets – neither yourself nor the audience).

Some performers – Graham P Jolley, as already noted – fall primarily into the aggressive camp, and attack the audience. Others, such as Ian Keable, whilst still 'aggressive', have a more self-deprecating approach and attack both the audience and themselves. Yet others – Tommy Cooper is probably one of the best examples – opt for a largely 'funny' approach that tries to avoid targets altogether. (Or, if not, as in Tommy's case, target themselves.)

Decide which type of performer you are, and concentrate your fire in that direction.

4. Humour (in) your props

If your act uses props – and most acts do – think of ways of adapting or distorting them.   Exaggeration is a great comic tool.   Mel Mellers, for example, uses a very large pencil in his act, to great comic effect.   You might choose to use large cards that you are patently unable to shuffle, or – for an audience of magicians, perhaps – a giant sponge ball it's impossible to palm.   Equally, you might go to the other extreme and make something much smaller than usual. As mentioned (see p 3), in the right circumstances, shuffling a tiny deck of cards might evoke laughter because it's unusual – incongruous even.   Whatever your approach, exaggeration is a tried-and-tested way to create humour.

John Archer has a terrific visual prop that begins as a play on words but ends as an amusing sight gag. He tells the audience he made a name for himself in woodwork. He then displays a wooden frame which bears his name.   He has – literally – made a name for himself.

Once, during a drawing duplication effect, I saw a magician tell the audience he wouldn't attempt to peek at his helper's drawing because that would be cheating. He then produced a telescopic rod from his pocket to which he had attached a small mirror.   With his back to the helper, he fed the rod high into the air. There was no way this piece of equipment could aid him, but because it was an unexpected – and frankly daft – prop, it got the laughs he was hoping for.

5. Laughter is contagious

Sigmund Freud once wrote, 'The most favourable condition for comic pleasure is a generally happy disposition in which one is in the mood for laughter.' He went on to say that once we're in that mood, almost anything will make us laugh. 'We laugh at the expectation of laughing, at the appearance of one who is presenting the comic material (sometimes even before he attempts to make us laugh), and, finally, we laugh at the recollection of having laughed.'

You may not want your audience laughing throughout as it'll distract from the magic – but if you can generate a 'happy disposition', the laughs will come that much easier.

6. Be yourself; avoiding clichés

There are many clichéd lines in magic. I certainly don't want to suggest you ignore a good joke if it gets you laughs – even, perhaps, a joke that people are familiar with. That said, the more original you are, the more you set yourself apart from others in your field. Our profession is packed with clones. The jokes and patter that come with a merchandised trick – DVD versions, in particular – often appear to be 'just right'. The performer gets a powerful reaction, and we believe we will, too. So we leave it at that and perform our magic like everyone else.

At times, the industry exhorts us to be unoriginal. Hilarious performers release DVDs of their acts in which audience members are all but carried out on stretchers at the end of each routine. These performers are often genuinely very funny and have worked hard to create a strong, amusing act. But their routines work because they are born out of character (see p 4). For most of us, many of their jokes, their patter, and much of their idiosyncratic approach are, to all intents and purposes, worthless. Not because they don't work. On the contrary, they usually work very well indeed. But the humour used doesn't reflect our character and, when we attempt the same jokes, they fall flat. We know it, and, more importantly, the audience knows it.

We know that using someone else's approach to a trick can sometimes suck the life from it. We're treading in their footsteps, but we're not them. It doesn't feel right. When we use our own storyline, we make the trick more our own and feel more comfortable with it. It's the same with humour. Write and use your own lines, and you make the act your own. That way, you present more of yourself on stage, which is never a bad thing.

It's fine if you're acting a role and it's carefully defined, practised and one with which you're comfortable and familiar. But, for most of us, the best and easiest approach to adopt on stage is to be ourselves – or a best/worst/exaggerated version of ourselves. If we use other people's lines, we risk losing that special something that makes us unique.

Of course, clichés *can* be a source of humour. Many jokes are nothing more than an opening, familiar straight line, followed by a humorous pay-off.

The following joke, for example, pokes fun at the magician's tendency to over-spend at conventions:

> 'A fool and his money ... *are welcome at every dealer stand in Blackpool.'*

If you want quick practice in gag-writing, make a list of straight lines – catchphrases, proverbs, idioms and the like – and let your imagination wander. It's amazing where it can lead you.

7. Gag-writing methods

In general, magic does not lend itself to irrelevant storytelling. I'm not talking about talented people like Lesley Melville, whose stories can illustrate and enhance their magic. What I mean is: most magicians are unlikely to find themselves announcing that their next piece of skulduggery involves 'an Englishman, an Irishman and a Scotsman'.

As I've indicated in the Introduction, these notes are not meant to provide an in-depth analysis of comedy-writing techniques. (For works that cover this area in much more detail, see the Bibliography at the end of this book.) However, let me give you a few examples of methods and how you might use them to create your own gags.

Exaggeration

This is one of the easiest gag-writing methods around. At its simplest, in order to exaggerate something, you associate it with something else.

For example:

> 'We have a magician in our club – his tricks are so long, they'd take half an hour to go through a five-minute car wash.'

What you've done here is to take one idea – the length of a performer's act – and associate it with something else (a car wash) that involves time passing. By linking the two, you create a gag.

Similarly:

> 'His act is so long, he not only sells tickets – he offers bed and breakfast.'

Here, the idea is that the act is so long, you have to stay overnight to watch it all.

Taking the same approach, you might – in politically incorrect fashion – decide to emphasise how large your mother-in-law is. To use an old joke as an example:

> 'My mother-in-law is huge. She was on the bus last week. Four men got up to offer her a seat. If two more had done it, she could have accepted.'

Here, we've taken the idea of a person's size and, instead of simply saying she's big and leaving it at that, we've said, 'She's the size of six grown men.'

If you want to create a visual gag, then you might physically exaggerate the shape or size of a prop.   As already mentioned, if you exaggerate the size of playing cards, for example – whether using A4-size or miniature – it's possible to engineer a situation in which the use of such cards is visually amusing.

Similarly, a giant sponge ball that can't be palmed, or a huge drinking straw emerging from a paper bag, is funny, in part because we don't expect it, and in part because it is not as it ought to be.

Word play

This is another relatively easy gag-writing method.

John Archer's 'I made a name for myself' (p 6) is an example of word play being used to create a visual gag. More commonly, however, in word play, you lead the audience to believe you are using an expression in one sense, before revealing that you actually mean something very different.

To take another old joke:

> 'I almost didn't get here tonight. I had a breakdown on the way to the show. I don't know what happened – I just burst into tears.'

The key word here is 'breakdown', which, in the usual context, we take to mean a mechanical fault of some kind. But 'breakdown' has more than one meaning.   When we reveal the meaning we really intend, it's unexpected (a surprise – one of the funny bone's trigger points), and we laugh.

Here's a similar gag where we deliberately misinterpret the meaning of the word 'sentence':

> The judge said, 'I'm going to give you a long sentence.' The prisoner replied, 'I don't mind – as long as you speak slowly.'

So look for alternative meanings to words and phrases. Ask yourself: what else might this mean? The more alternatives you can find, the more jokes you'll come up with.

The simple truth

The simple truth gag is a variant of word play. Here, your set-up is a broad statement of fact, and your punch line a valid comment/consequence/observation. There is generally a literal truth to the punch line – something that the audience will recognise as being a perfectly acceptable (and humorous) interpretation of the facts.

For example, to take another old joke:

> 'An accountant is someone who tells you exactly how much money you have. And how much of it you owe to him.'

In essence, what you're saying here is: an accountant is expensive. He will analyse your financial position but he will charge you a lot of money for the privilege. (Many good jokes are nothing more than everyday observations cloaked in humour.)

To construct the joke, you make a list of ideas/concepts/words etc connected with accountancy, then relate one or more of these to the original statement. Your list might include: inland revenue, invoices, tax demands, allowances, numbers, fees, audit, profit and loss, end-of-year returns, book-keeping, double-entries, and so on.

Examine the words you've come up and look for the 'hidden funny'. What else might a word/phrase mean? Might it link to some other subject? Looking at 'tax demands', for example, might lead you onto a different subject altogether. Thus, one simple truth gag (albeit unrelated to accountants) might be:

> 'Being a tax inspector is a very *demanding* job. Especially come April the fifth [*ie the end of the tax year*]...'

'Double entries', meanwhile, is the sort of phrase that screams 'innuendo'. (As an exercise, give it a go if you like!)

Approaching the joke as written, we'd look at the prospect of 'fees'. An accountant's fees are generally on the high side, which means we'll be handing over money to him as well as the tax man. By relating that idea (ie how much you'll owe the accountant) to the opening statement (ie how much money you have) the joke all but writes itself.

Adopting a similar approach, and with different professions in mind, you might come up with the following:

A policeman is someone who tells you the time – *and how much of it you're likely to serve for wasting his.*

A lawyer will defend you from villains. *Generally, other lawyers.*

A banker will look after money on your behalf, invest it on your behalf, *and then spend it on your behalf.*

A boxer is someone who hits you for money – *much like the taxman.*

Let's use the above approach with a magician in mind. Opening with the assumption that our magician is successful. we might say:

'Wherever he performs, people queue up to buy tickets.'

That's a straightforward, easy-to-understand statement. Now examine it. Ask yourself as many questions about it as possible. What do we mean by 'performs'? Where do people queue? What sort of people? Why do they queue? What sort of tickets might they be queuing for?

Ask yourself if any words can be replaced. Are there any sound-a-like words? (Ie homonyms.) 'Queue' sounds like 'cue'. 'Buy' sounds like 'bye'. 'People' sounds like 'peep-hole'. It doesn't matter how daft – or apparently useless – the answers to your questions are, this is an information-gathering exercise.

Let's look at the questions 'Why do they queue?' and 'What sort of tickets might they be queuing for?' The obvious

14

answer is: they're queuing for tickets to the show. But what if they were queuing for other tickets? What other tickets do people queue for? Well, among other things, they queue for railway, bus and airline tickets. Ie, tickets to 'get away somewhere'.

Using this idea, we might come up with the following line:

'Wherever he performs, people queue up to buy tickets. *The bus station, the railway station, the airport. They don't care where they go ...'*

This statement confounds expectations. It's a *surprise* conclusion which suggests the performer isn't as good as he thinks he is. (And is, of course, an example of the *insult* joke.) Whilst the line as written would suit a compere, it could easily be reworded for use by the magician himself.

For example:

'Wherever I perform, people queue up to buy tickets. *The bus station, the railway station, the airport. They don't care where they go ...'*

One popular joke-writing formula is the 'question and answer' approach. For example, 'What do you call a ...', 'Why is one thing like another?' and so on.

List as many ordinary day-to-day situations as possible and ask yourself how they might apply to magicians (or any other category you'd like to poke fun at). Here, you're not only looking for a readily identifiable set of circumstances, but an inherent weakness/characteristic that leads to a humorous but logical conclusion. For example:

'Why do magicians crash their cars so often? *Because they never know when to stop.'*

In conclusion, when constructing a 'simple truth' gag, begin with a straightforward statement of fact – a cliché, if you like. Your conclusion should be an unexpected, but realistic, interpretation of that statement. Look for alternative meanings and ask as many questions of the statement as you possibly can.

Insult

Insults can be aimed at all manner of targets, but for the purposes of magic we'll restrict ourselves to people or props. Insult humour is basically a form of attack – a hostile remark aimed at a specific target. Thus, one example might be:

'Magic is a dying art. *At least it is the way I perform it.'*

Here, we take a clichéd expression: '[*Something*] is a dying art' and apply it to magic. We then ask ourselves: how could this be rewritten so that we attack something or someone?

To create the joke we ask: 'How might someone (in this case, a magician) contribute to magic as a dying art?' Answer: *by performing it*. The thinking behind this is that he will do it so badly, it will put even more people off and hasten its demise.

That's a clinical way of dissecting the joke – but often an insult joke is built around a very dull, straightforward remark.

Again, to quote an old favourite:

'I see you went to the hairdressers, madam. What a shame they were closed.'

To construct this joke, you start with a bald statement (no pun intended!): 'Madam, your hair is a mess.' You then ask yourself: 'Why would it be a mess?' Search out as many answers as possible; the more answers you come up with, the greater your chances of creating an original joke.

An obvious reason, of course, is that the lady has not been to the hairdressers. However, 'Your hair is a mess, madam, what a shame you didn't go the hairdressers' is not a funny line.

Let's assume she did go. What outcomes does this provide us with? Listing possibilities, we might come up with the following: (a) while at the hairdressers, something awful happened; (b) while at the hairdressers, she asked for a style that didn't suit her; (c) she got there, but they were shut.

Starting with the third possibility, ie option (c) above, we come up with the joke as written.

But let's look at option (a), ie something awful happened. What might that awful thing have been? If her hair is a mess, perhaps it was cut by a really bad hairdresser? Or maybe she asked for a particular style?

Reaching these conclusions gives you more joke-writing possibilities. What if the hairdresser was disadvantaged in some way? This might lead to:

'I see you went to the hairdressers, madam. Very nice. [*Apparently changing the subject*] Care in the community is a wonderful thing, isn't it? [*Addressing the lady again*] But they really shouldn't let them loose with scissors.'

I'm not suggesting this is hilarious, nor that it's the sort of joke I would tell – but I hope it helps show you how you might construct this type of gag.

Finally, what about option (b) – ie the lady had asked for a style that doesn't suit her? Here, we would be looking to compare the style with something else. Maybe a celebrity who is known for a wild look.

For example:

'What lovely hair, madam. I see the Ken Dodd look is back in this year.'

Recycling material

Take an existing joke and tailor it to your situation. For example:

'I was asked if I'd like to give ten quid towards a lawyer's funeral. I said, "Here's a hundred – bury ten of them".'

18

This could be rewritten to play on a magician's prejudice:

'I got a letter from the Conjurers' Welfare Fund last week. They asked me for £5 towards a sponge ball magician's funeral. I sent them 50 quid. I said, "Bury ten of them."'

The following 'laughing at men' joke:

'What do you call 144 blokes in a room? *Gross stupidity.*'

could be rewritten to replace 'blokes' with anyone you'd like to poke fun at. Equally, you could take the 'gross stupidity' punch line and look for similar phrases such as 'gross indecency'. This could give you the line:

'What do you call 144 flashers in a room? *Gross indecency.*'

There are no end of 'slim book' jokes such as:

'What's the slimmest book in the world? *What Men Know About Women.*'

This could be rewritten to poke fun at the magician's tendency to 'over-perform'. Thus:

'What the slimmest book in the world? *Tricks a Card Magician Won't Show You.*'

I'm sure you get the idea by now. Hunt down jokes that lend themselves to rewriting, and, if possible, alter them to suit your purpose or situation.

What else might it mean?

This is a rich source of humour – examples of which I have already given.

Let me provide a few more, analysing them briefly as we go:

> 'I watched a magician saw a woman in half last night. *It wasn't part of his act, she just annoyed him.'*

Here, we take a cliché, 'A magician saws a woman in half', and ask ourselves: why might he do this? The obvious answer is: it's part of his act. But why else might he do it? Well, he might do it if he were a psychopath and she gave him a hard time: outlandish and unlikely, perhaps, but an amusing – and logical – conclusion.

Again, more self-deprecating this time:

> 'Magic helps pay my bills. *But only if I sell my props.'*

Analysis: The first part of the joke is, once again, a straight, believable line. The implication is that the speaker makes money by performing magic. But what else could it mean? How else might a magician make money? Well, we all have a huge amount of magic hiding away in our cupboards – and selling it would raise cash. Though selling props isn't intrinsically funny, the thought that the only way a magician can make money is by selling his props is an amusing image, albeit one that relies on attacking the magician's competence.

> 'Magic isn't real, of course. *Well – not the way I perform it.'*

Analysis: Once again, we begin with a straight line, 'Magic isn't real.' Then we ask ourselves why it couldn't or might not be real. One answer would be that, much as in a poorly acted play, the performance detracts from the reality – which leads us quickly to the punch line.

In similar vein, here's another self-deprecating remark:

> 'I asked two people to help me with this trick last night. *But they didn't know how to do it, either.'*

Analysis: The straight line lends itself to more than one interpretation. The obvious conclusion is that the magician simply requires helpers to carry out his effect. But another meaning might be: he needs help because he has no idea how the trick works.

Finally:

> 'His act is so bad, he does the bullet catch – *whether he likes it or not.'*

Analysis: The bullet catch is a cliché of magic. In performing it, a gun is fired at the magician. Ask yourself: why else might someone fire a gun at a magician? Answer: because he's so bad they want to kill him.

Playing with clichés

A cliché is often a perfectly valid statement we've simply heard too many times. Magicians are always using them.

As I've remarked elsewhere (see p 8), by taking a familiar statement and using it as a take-off point for a joke, clichés can be a rich source of humour.

But that aside, there are lots of clichéd comic lines in magic. Some argue it doesn't matter. The lines may be old hat to magicians, but lay audiences have never heard them before. I'm not convinced. People have heard far more than we sometimes give them credit for. And even if they haven't, using the same old lines again and again is lazy (even if they work).

As an exercise, take as many clichéd lines as possible and see if you can come up with something better – or at least something that works for you. To take a few examples:

'Make your mind go blank – that was fast.'

or

'Have we met before?'

'No.'

'Then how do you know it's me?'

or

'Have we met before?'

'No.'

'You look rather happy about that.'

or

'Give me your hand. No, the clean one.'

First off, ask yourself: what am I trying to say? In the opening example ('Make your mind go blank') – which clearly falls under the heading of 'Insult' humour and won't be to everyone's taste – we're effectively saying that our helper has an empty mind. Not to put too fine a point on it, he or she is vacant, possibly even a bit thick. Though you may not mean anything by it, the remark is potentially offensive.

So why not think about shifting the object of derision? And where better to shift it than in the direction of one of our overpaid celebrities/politicians and/or other public figures we love to hate? (Another example of humour, which remains perennially popular!)

If you want to use a joke that depends on someone having a certain quality (eg a vacant mind) ask yourself who is known for that? Well, at the time of writing, Wayne Rooney is a celebrity generally – if unfairly – seen as fitting that bill. And 'Britain's Got Talent' judge, Amanda Holden is probably not far behind.

With this as your starting-point, you might come up with something like:

'Make your mind a blank. If it helps, imagine you're Wayne Rooney.' (*Or, if you're talking to a woman,* 'Victoria Beckham/Amanda Holden'.)

If self-deprecation is your style, you might choose to go with:

'Make your mind a blank. If it helps, imagine you're me.'

While on this subject, never forget that really useful catch-all punch line. If you make a statement that's potentially ambiguous and people laugh, sometimes all you need to say, to get yet another laugh, is: 'You're writing your own jokes now.' It can sometimes be as simple as that.

But still on the subject of clichés, let's look at the 'Have we met before?' jokes. Again, what are we trying to say? Well, basically, we're remarking on all the possible reactions people might have on meeting us. Sometimes, people are pleased to meet us, sometimes they're not.

Before writing the joke, ask yourself: *where do I want to direct my humour?*

Insult magicians direct their humour at the one person who deserves it least – the person who's helping them. If this is your preferred approach, then your target is your helper. But there are other targets, most notably ourselves. I appreciate self-deprecating humour is not to everyone's taste, either, and certainly doesn't suit some characters. As I've already remarked, Graham P Jolley's persona would lack credibility if he spent half his time attacking himself.

24

But let's say *we* are the target and assume the helper isn't pleased to see us. It's completely ruined their day. This is the thinking behind the response, 'You look rather happy about that.'

Ask yourself, 'What other ways are there of saying the same thing?' You may come up with a better line, you may not. But whatever line you do come up with, it will be yours.

Possible responses (to a presumed 'No' reply') might be:

(a)   It's your lucky day.   Or at least it was.   [Self-deprecating]

(b)   You don't have to say it like that. [Self-deprecating]

(c)   [Risque – with a man, and depending on your own approach.]   But it's a pleasure, isn't it?   [*Looking at his trousers*] I can tell.

Finally, how might we approach the insult line, 'Give me your hand. No, the clean one'?

As with all jokes, begin with a list. Note down everything you can think of that relates to hands: big hands, small hands, manicured hands, hands of a clock, fingernails, wedding rings, gloves, knuckles, fingers, thumbs, lifelines and so on. Don't restrict or edit yourself.

Using the above list as a starting-point, let's investigate 'lifelines'. If we want to avoid insulting our helper, we might assume he or she has a long, healthy lifeline (something we all want to hear!).   At this point, we need to ask more questions. Why, for example, might someone have a long, healthy lifeline? The reason might be genetic, because they eat well, look after themselves and so on.

Let's go with the idea that they look after themselves. Perhaps they work out? 'Work out' is useful, because it's a phrase with alternative meanings.   Pursuing this approach, we might end up with something like:

> 'That's a healthy lifeline. You obviously work out. Let's hope you can't work out how this trick's done.'

Play around with ideas – and have fun!

8. Horses for courses

Humour for one audience may not necessarily work for another. Jokes that tickle the collective funny bone of an audience of lawyers wouldn't necessarily amuse a gathering of company salesmen. Using magicians as an example, a joke that refers to some aspect of conjuring might leave a lay audience completely unmoved. Thus:

> 'A fool and his money ... are welcome at every dealer stall in Blackpool'

might amuse magicians because it reminds us of how much money we've wasted over the years. It would obviously mean nothing to an audience of non-magicians.

If you are performing for magicians – in a competition, for example – make a list of words, character traits, activities and so on relevant to magicians, and use these as your starting-point for creating gags.

Let's say you want to come up with a joke about the classic force. There are two words in that description, 'classic' and 'force'. Ask yourself:

- Are there other meanings to these words?
- Are there other words that sound like these words?

Using this approach, you might consider the cultural interpretation of 'classic' and produce something along the following lines:

'He has a brilliant classic force. It doesn't matter which books he offers you, you always pick the Jane Austen.'

Alternatively, the word 'force' may remind you of 'farce', and you might go with:

'I'm not very good at card magic. To be honest, my classic force is more of a classic farce.'

But whatever the audience make-up, these approaches – making lists of key words/phrases, searching for alternative meanings and homonyms (words that sound or look like another word) – are very useful short-cuts to creating humour.

9. Sources of humour

One of the best sources of joke material is existing jokes. Buy a joke book, or write down jokes you hear and like. Make a list of visual jokes – especially ones used by successful magicians. Then play around with them. Use the set-up, but change the punch line. Or keep the punch line and change the set-up. Or go completely wild – and change both!

Again, look for formulae. There are plenty around. For example:

- 'How many [*insert relevant profession/character type*] does it take to change a light bulb?'
- 'What do you call a [*usually a man/woman/animal with certain characteristics*]?'
- 'Why is [*X*] like [*Y*]?'
- 'Blonde' jokes. [*But change 'blonde' to whoever you want to poke fun at.*]
- 'Why did the chicken cross the road?' [*But change 'chicken' to a different animal/person/profession etc.*]
- Englishman/Irishman and Scotsman jokes. [*But alter the parties to suit different people/professions etc.*]
- Definition jokes. [*Eg taking a phrase and redefining it, as in the 'gross stupidity' joke at p 19.*]

Not all formulae will be suitable, but, in trying them out, you'll exercise your funny bone. The more you practise, the easier you'll find it to write your own gags.

CONCLUSION

Joke-writing is fun, and there are many ways to go about writing gags, only a few of which I've been able to touch on here. To summarise:

- Ask yourself: how can I surprise someone; what would be out of place; how can I ratchet up the tension and then relieve it in a light-hearted way?

- Examine each word in a phrase/cliché/statement and look for alternative meanings.

- Ask yourself: what if? What if my props were larger/smaller/invisible? What if I couldn't do this trick? What if I dropped my cards? And so on. The more questions you ask, the more ammunition you will have for gag-writing.

- If you want to write jokes around a particular topic, make a list of everything you can think of connected to that topic: people, places, events, clichés, expressions etc. See if any of these ideas connect with each other.

- Use gag-writing techniques: exaggeration; insult; word play; topical (using items/stories/personalities currently in the news); simple truth; clichés.

- Go through a joke book or write out your favourite jokes and one-liners. Then 'parallel' those jokes. By that, I mean, write the same joke, but (a) keep the set-up and change the punch line; (b) keep the punch line but change the set-up; (c) change both the set-up and the punch line. You can do this for any type of joke. In doing so, you'll learn to unravel jokes and put them back together – but in a way that suits your own approach and personality.

Don't edit yourself until you're sure you've exhausted all the possibilities. Have fun!

JOKES

COMPERE

A few jokes for when you find yourself 'taking it easy' and hosting a show for others...

It's easy to get laughs by poking fun at someone's little faults. So let's get started on the people in the front row.

I spoke to a Liverpudlian last week about stereotypes in comedy. That was a mistake. He stole my entire act.

I compered a show at a Christian Yacht Club last month. They asked me to pepper my act with nautical jokes. I misheard them. I won't be working there again.

At my last show, someone yelled, 'Your act is a joke.' I said, 'Well, you're the one watching it.'

Someone yelled out, 'Tell us a joke!' I said, 'You're watching one. Is that not enough?'

Our next act is a man of many parts. Part man, part animal...

I was so bored, I didn't lose the will to live – I threw it away.

Our next act has performed all over the world. He has to, the police keep moving him on.

We booked a memory act for our show tonight – but he forgot to turn up.

We booked the invisible man for our show tonight. If you see him, let me know.

Wherever he performs, people queue up to buy tickets. The bus station, the railway station, the airport. They don't care where they go …

You look like a woman half your age. So what are you – 83?

I can't tell you how happy I am to be here tonight. Because I'm not.

Our next act is a mind-reader from Hull [*or name any place you think the audience will view as 'the enemy'*]. He's not very good. But then, to be fair, coming from Hull he's not had much chance to practise.

As a magician, our next act is without equal. Three thousand professional magicians in this country – and he's the worst one.

Our next act is a man who appeals to audiences everywhere he goes. Usually to let him out in one piece.

People kept asking me how I broke my arm. I told them I didn't. Someone else did. I'm not gigging there again ...

Our next act is wanted all over the country. You may have seen his posters at your local police station.

Our next act has appeared on television many times. 'News at Ten', 'Crimewatch', 'Rogue Traders'...

Our closing act this evening is highly sought after. Generally by the bailiffs.

Our next act dedicates his every waking hour to magic. He would have been on first, but he slept in.

Our next act is an illusionist. At least he'll try to convince you he's got a good act.

It is a two-way street, of course. Our acts tonight will perform to their absolute peak in an effort to bring you a class of entertainment you've never experienced before. But equally, you, for your part, must set your standards rather low.

Our next act tonight is one of the busiest magicians in the country. Unless, of course, there's anyone here from the Inland Revenue – in which case he hasn't worked for six months.

Our next act was big in variety in the 1950s, even bigger on television in the 1970s. Tonight – he's absolutely enormous. Will you please put your hands together for ...

I've seen our next act several times over the years. And take it from me – he hasn't got any better.

Our next act has worked in some of the finest theatres in the country. So if you want an ice cream in the interval, you know who to look for.

Our next act has delighted audiences all over the world. Usually by not turning up.

As you know, we only book the finest acts money can buy. So tonight, for 23p …

Our next act has not only made people believe in the afterlife – it's encouraged them to go looking for it.

An act like the next one comes along just once in a lifetime. So take heart, it'll never happen again …

There's nothing I can say about this act … without being sued for libel.

Paul Daniels once voted our next act the most entertaining magician he'd ever seen. Then the drugs wore off and he just screamed.

We searched far and wide for our next act … because he has a habit of wandering off. Especially after … you know … [*mime drinking*]

Our next act is a man to keep your eye on ... especially if you've brought your wife along.

Our next act is a man to keep your eye on. And that's not just my view – the police have issued warnings, too.

I saw our next act in the dressing room before the show. He said, 'I can't go on.' 'I said, 'What – no confidence?' He said, 'No – no trousers.' Unfortunately for us, he's found a pair. Ladies and gentlemen ... *Etc.*

I'd like to thank you all for turning up tonight because – let's be honest – it's always a bit disheartening performing to an empty room. But enough of my last show ...

He's a full-time professional magician which is why, in this current economic climate, he can be with us tonight.

They say the best things in life are free – which is why you had to pay to come in tonight.

Our first act needs no introduction, but he's given me one anyway. [*Unroll long paper scroll. The gag can end there or you can continue as follows:*] I can't read that. No, really, I can't. It's in Chinese. Look, see... [*Turn it round to reveal lots of Chinese lettering*]

I'd like to conclude tonight's proceedings with some wise words from the ancient Chinese philosopher, Confucius. [*Make jokey-type Chinese sounds*] I've no idea what it means, either. But you've been a lovely audience. Thank you and good night.

He's a member of The Tragic Circle. You think I've made a mistake there for comic purposes, but wait till you see him perform.

No I'm only kidding. He is a member of The Magic Circle, the International Brotherhood of Magicians and the AA. And when I tell you he doesn't drive a car, you can draw your own conclusions about that last bit.

MAGICIANS

Jokes and lines for when you're performing – whether in a show, a competition, for friends or just some poor soul you've stopped in the street...

This is a completely true story. Apart from the bits I've made up.

You're not going to believe this. And why should you? It's not true ...

Ten years ago, I took a vow of poverty. I became a children's entertainer.

The top minds in magic said this next trick couldn't be done. And do you know what? They were right.

This is the best trick in the world. Not the way I perform it, obviously.

When I finish, people burst into wild, spontaneous applause. It's nothing to do with the magic, they're just glad to see the back of me.

A wise man once said, 'The successful magician knows when to—'

I'm just back from a week in Las Vegas, where I headlined with the most famous singer in the world, Lady Gaga. Admittedly, the headline was 'British man stalks mad American bird'. But all publicity is good publicity – though apparently that isn't a valid defence in a court of law.

I actually flew to Las Vegas with Ryanair. Interesting place, Las Vegas. Someone asked me how I found it. I said fortunately I didn't have to – the pilot knew the way.

Ryanair are well-known for their money-making scams. A while back they tried to charge every passenger an extra £5 to use their toilet. Or – to give it its technical term – Ryanair.

But to be fair, and I didn't know this until recently, on Ryanair, for an extra £10 you can upgrade … to economy class.

Tonight, I shall be performing the most dangerous trick in the world. Because if you don't like it … you'll probably kill me.

I've performed in some rough places. So tonight doesn't hold any fears for me.

[*When mindreading*] I'd like you to imagine a location anywhere in the world. I'm getting emptiness, desolation ... no, wait a minute that's my social life.

I will now perform the one illusion the great Houdini was unable to. Owing largely to the fact that it was invented after he died.

I haven't always been a magician. To be fair, some people say I'm not one now.

For my next trick, I need a lady volunteer. But I don't want to force anyone. If you'd rather not help, just stand up now ... and rip all your clothes off.

I was heckled last night. By the crowd in a club next door.

I saw a terrific magician last week. He said we should all help each other. So I've helped myself to his act.

I haven't been a full-time magician for very long. [*Glance at watch.*] Just over two minutes to be precise.

Did you hear about the fisherman who took up magic? He was always asking people to 'Pick a cod, any cod.'

Did you hear about the secret agent who took up magic? He was always asking people to 'Pick a code, any code.'

Here's a contradiction in terms: 'I took up magic for a living.'

God works in mysterious ways. Much like a sponge ball magician.

They say Harry Potter has some good ideas. Personally, I don't think he lives in the real world.

The Magic Circle described me as 'The Man of the Moment'. Unfortunately, that moment was three years ago…

The thing about being a magician is: if you can make just one trick work really well; if you can make just one trick the best an audience has ever seen; if you can make just one trick something an audience will talk about for weeks afterwards … then you have a very short act.

Mentalists distort reality. Well, they certainly make time pass more slowly.

Guy Hollingworth is funny, clever, handsome, intelligent, inventive and one of the most skilful magicians in the world. Other than that, he doesn't impress me at all.

Every magician knows a thousand card tricks. And if you're really lucky – he won't show you any.

He's such a bad magician – he passed the audition for our magic club.

Am I the only one who thinks Paul Curry's best card trick was Out of This World?

I used to do Professor's Nightmare. But not very well. It was a bit of a ropey act.

Did you hear about the lovesick magician? He wasn't looking for Miss Right, he was looking for Miss Direction.

He's a crafty magician. He never misses a trick.

There are two types of conjuror in the average magic society. Bad ones – and really bad ones.

David Blaine drove past me last week. He had this big sign in the rear window: 'Magicians do it with their wands.'

I bumped into the Masked Magician last week. I say 'bumped'; it was more of a punch to the throat, really. [*Alter the name to anyone else who's none too popular.*]

The first trick I bought, the dealer said, 'This is a real reputation maker.' He was right. After I performed it, I didn't work again for two years.

How do you torture a magician? Nail his hands to a wall and beg him to show you a card trick.

Card magicians never die. They just shuffle off.

I said to him, 'If you were me, how would you perform this trick?' He said, 'Better.'

Someone once asked me, 'Have you ever died on stage'? I said, 'Died, been buried, dug up again and had a stake rammed through the heart.' I'm not doing [name any venue or club] again...

I don't rehearse. Rehearsal is for wimps. Successful wimps, mind...

His act is so bad, he does the bullet catch whether he likes it or not.

He does magic down the pub. Every time it's his round he disappears.

His act goes down a bomb – at least the place looks like one hit it wherever he performs.

He was once arrested for performing at the London Palladium. Mind you, he wasn't actually in the show at the time.

His act was so bad, he heckled himself.

He's the man who puts the 'slight' into sleight of hand.

The act on before me so was so bad – they were still booing him after I finished.

Magic isn't real, of course. Well, not the way I perform it.

Magic helps me pay the bills. But only if I sell my props.

Magic has brought me a lot of happiness. Which is more than can be said for my audiences.

My last audience called me back on stage for an encore. They wanted to boo me in a different language.

When I perform, I'm often paid £500 a show. To leave early.

He has a tendency to antagonise his audiences. Generally by starting his act.

At my last show I asked two people to help me with this next trick. But they didn't know how to do it, either.

I cut a lady in half last night. It wasn't part of the act, she just annoyed me.

If at first you don't succeed, don't try the bullet catch.

They say magic is a dying art. Well, it is the way I perform it.

A fool and his money – are welcome at every dealer stand in Blackpool.

He has a brilliant classic force. It doesn't matter which book he offers you, you always choose the Jane Austen.

The Magic Circle sent me a letter asking if I'd like to give five quid towards a card magician's funeral. I said, 'Here's a hundred, bury 20 of them.'

I've just bought a new DVD – 'Easy To Master Escapology'. Unfortunately, I can't get the wrapper off.

When I started out, I was a bad magician. But after years of practice, I'm now a really bad one.

He's a bad magician. He robs banks.

He made small objects disappear. I tried – but I couldn't Toppit.

Escapologists are born free – but everywhere they are in chains.

What's the difference between a magician and a bus driver? The bus driver knows when to stop.

As a working magician, you sometimes have to associate with unsavoury people. Other magicians, mostly.

You've got to laugh. I wish you would.

You've got to laugh. Well, some of you have to – I paid you when you came in.

Do you know the difference between a good magician and a bad magician? No? That's a relief.

[Consulting some notes] For my next trick, I need a right pair. [Consulting them again] I'm sorry, I need a perfect couple.

[IN A COMPETITION] I love competitions like this. People are always so friendly. The other contestants have been giving me lots of advice. Things like, 'Go home, loser, you're rubbish.'

[IN A COMPETITION] I'd like to begin with a prediction. I'm not going to win tonight.

[IN A COMPETITION] If you liked my act, I've been [your name]. If you didn't, I've been [another act].

[IN A COMPETITION] How many magicians does it take to change a light bulb? I don't know – I haven't bought the Alakazam DVD.

[IN A COMPETITION] How do avoid a bore at a magicians' convention? Don't go.

I've never performed comedy magic before. And I'm not sure I'm doing it now.

I did a show a few weeks back. Afterwards, a woman said to my wife, 'That's the funniest thing I've ever seen.' My wife said, 'My husband's act?' She said, 'No – your husband.'

[When using two people] This trick only works when a couple are deeply in love. So if it goes wrong, we know who to blame.

I saw my doctor this morning. He said, 'If I were you I wouldn't perform tonight.' I said, 'Why not – dodgy heart?' He said, 'No. Dodgy act.'

After my last show, a woman came up to me and said, 'That's the funniest thing I've ever seen.' I said, 'You liked my act?' She said, 'No, your flies were undone.'

Scientists in America have crossed a card magician with a stripper. And come up with a man who can bore the pants off himself.

I haven't done this trick before. So if it goes wrong, I'll never know.

Believe it or not, sir, I have now controlled your card ... to a completely unknown part of the deck.

They say you should open with your best trick. That way you grab the audience. I've never known why. Let's face it – it's all downhill after that.

Why did the magician cross the road? Because all the other magicians were doing it.

What do you call a magician who won't show you a card trick? The deceased.

I love statistics almost as much as I love magic. Did you know: in the last 30 minutes, Wayne Rooney has made £1000, 800 babies have been born ... and Jay Sankey has released twelve DVDs.

When I was a child my mother asked me what I wanted to be when I grew up. I said, 'A magician.' She said, 'Make up your mind, you can't do both.'

I said to my wife, 'You know, I've half a mind to become a professional magician'. She said, 'That should do.'

I was chatting to another magician the other day. He said, 'My father was a traffic warden.' I said, 'That's a coincidence. My dad didn't know his father, either.'

I stood up on stage last night, the audience went wild. Like a pack of bloody wolves, they were. I tell you, I got out of there fast.

At my last show, someone asked, 'When did you take up magic?' I said, 'Ten years ago.' He said, 'And when will you be showing us some?'

MISCELLANEOUS

Jokes for every occasion. Or none at all...

I went down the pub last night. Whole thing was up on stilts. I said to the landlord, 'What's that all about?' He said, 'I'm raising the bar.'

Once upon a time, on a planet, in a galaxy, far, far away ... nothing happened. They never tell you that story, do they?

My brother winds up clocks. He tells them they're running late when they're not.

Until the year 1973, I'd never lost money on the horses. Then I took up gambling.

I studied philosophy at college. I was a follower of the sceptics – who believe we can never be certain of anything. But these days, I'm not so sure.

When I won the Lottery, my neighbours sent me begging letters. They begged me to use the money to move somewhere else.

They say, 'Quit while you're ahead.' Where does that leave elbows?

They say the best men are all married – which isn't what their wives think.

He said, 'Our kitchen floors are so clean, you could eat your dinner off them.' I said, 'I know – I've just seen two cockroaches having a right old feast.'

A friend of mine had a problem with his bowels. He swallowed three cogs and a couple of springs. Now he's as regular as clockwork.

I went to see my doctor this morning. He said, 'Do you take vigorous exercise first thing in the morning?' I said, 'Well, I force myself out of bed.'

My mate's so unlucky. He's never even had a winning smile.

There are some things I don't do as I get older. I don't sharpen pencils for a start. Well, I don't see the point.

My brother went to see every musical in London's west end. Then came back and gave me a show-by-show account.

The Society for Really Angry People held their annual convention last week. They only booked half a theatre. They were able to fill it up though – because they were all beside themselves.

My wife has an hour-glass figure. Unfortunately, all her sand has dropped to the bottom.

My girlfriend asked me to name the day. I named it Fred. Stupid, I know – but that's women for you.

A man with a large Rolex thinks he's important, but really he's just got too much time on his hands.

I've made up my mind to be more decisive in future. No I haven't.

I've a very religious friend. He never plays golf on the Sabbath. Well, he doesn't like driving on a Sunday.

I woke up early this morning. He works nights, so he wasn't best pleased.

A friend of mine told me he had a bad accident. As opposed to what – the good kind?

Our house burnt down at the weekend. The oven caught fire. It was my wife's fault. She let me in the kitchen.

I went to see my doctor. He said, 'Fred [*or whatever your name is*], you've got the body of a 20-year-old.' To be fair, this was 30 years ago. [*Alter the ages to whatever suits you best.*]

I broke my arm twice. I'd have broken it three times – but fortunately someone stopped me.

Did you hear about the gambler who fell down the stairs – and broke even? [*Think*] No, wait a minute, he broke everything.

I told my wife I was taking up comedy for a living. She said, 'I hope you're joking.'

I told my wife I was taking up taxidermy for a living. She said, 'We're stuffed.'

Why do people say someone has the luck of the devil? Banished from paradise and made to sit in a fiery furnace for all eternity with a fork up his bottom. You wouldn't want to be him on a bad day, would you?

My uncle owned a toilet manufacturing business. Then the recession came along and it all went down the pan.

My uncle's a successful tree surgeon. He's just opened three new branches.

My brother rowed for Oxford. Well, he set off in the general direction...

I had an unhappy childhood. I never knew my mother. She left home before I was born.

Scientists have crossed a racing pigeon with a mallet. And come up with a bird that can hammer itself home.

My brother is the world's laziest chef. Always coming up with half-baked ideas.

They say accidents will happen. In which case – is it an accident?

Scientists have crossed a detective with a Thespian and come up with a man who can always catch himself in the act.

Someone once told my wife she should act her age. So she pretended she was 29.

She said to me, 'If you're the answer to a maiden's prayer, I'm sorry I asked the question.'

He was so unlucky ... he choked to death on a fortune cookie.

My teacher told me she thought I could go places. I said, 'What, like a scientist?' She said, 'No, like a courier.'

I've only argued with my wife once. I learned my lesson after that.

My wife said we should go somewhere different for our holidays. So we did. She went to Tenerife and I stayed at home.

I have a friend who hates flying. I told him: then stop waving your arms around so much!

They say what doesn't kill you makes you stronger. I was shot in the back last week. This week – amazing – never felt better.

The credit crunch reminds us there are three ways to live: sensibly, frugally or as if there's no tomorrow – which there possibly isn't.

Ed Miliband says he looks in the mirror every morning and sees a future prime minister. He keeps a photo of Yvette Cooper stuck in the corner. [*This is the sort of joke that can be updated/altered as necessary.*]

My brother was sent to prison for writing a letter. Well, to be fair it was several letters. One after another, on a wall, telling David Cameron where he could shove Nick Clegg. [*Again, the sort of joke that can be updated/altered as necessary.*]

Man went into the bank and said, 'I'd like to borrow £100.' The manager said, 'Why?' He said, 'Because I'm thinking of joining the Labour Party.' The manager said, 'That's a hefty subscription.' The man said, 'It's not a subscription, it's a doctor's fee. I need to get my head examined.' [*Again, change name of party/organisation to suit.*]

After a pretty, shapely young woman was mugged in the street, she was helped by a plain-clothes policeman – who turned out to be nothing of the sort. When the case came up in court, the judge asked, 'When did you first suspect the accused was not a policeman after all?' She thought about it for a moment, then said, 'When he dusted me for fingerprints.'

They say the family pet can often warn you when an earthquake's about to hit. It's true. We had a tremor at six o'clock this morning, and last night my budgie told me not to start any long novels.

My wife says I never show her a good time, so last week I took her to a car boot sale. She didn't like it, but she fetched three quid so it wasn't a total waste.

My wife ran off with a dwarf. Poor bugger was too small to fight her off.

She said, 'I wouldn't have married you if I'd known you weren't going places.' I said, 'It's only since I married you I've wanted to go places.'

Money can't buy you happiness. But if you're a woman, it can buy you a ton of shoes – and they'll do the job instead.

I bought an anti-gravity chair last week. What a waste of money. It just sits there …

When it drops below minus ten degrees, does a nudist camp put up a sign that says, 'We're clothed'?

Where do dwarves like to do their shopping? Lidl!

I've been learning German. I went into the pub and said, 'I'll have a lager, bitte'. The landlord said, 'Make up your mind.'

Talking of the future – which we'll come to in a minute.

I said to Ken Dodd, 'What's the secret of comedy?' He said, 'I'm not telling you.'

Say what you like about kerb-crawlers – at least they drive slowly.

Did you hear about the kerb-crawler who was fined for speeding? Apparently he was looking for fast women.

Did you hear about the bachelor comic? He only wrote single entendres.

He's a cross-country skier. Every time he goes skiing – he loses his temper.

Why don't the Mafia assassinate blondes? Because they never know too much.

I've got a friend, so nervous – he wears a parachute if he has to step off a kerb.

At Christmas, I throw salt and pepper over the postman and yell, 'Condiments of the season!'

I tried following her train of thought – but I had to get off at too many stations.

To solve pollution in cities we need to reinvent the wheel. Only this time it'll be square and made of concrete so it can't go anywhere.

I was in Berlin last week. Had a nasty turn, fell over. Fortunately, a German Good Samaritan stopped to help me. He said, 'No need to worry now – you're in safe Hans.'

My mother-in-law's never had a bad word to say for me. Two, three, often several dozen at a time. But never just the one.

The wife's mother was at death's door. But unfortunately they wouldn't let her in.

The condemned man was so superstitious – he asked if they'd mind not hanging him on Friday the 13th.

If you were to fire Nick Clegg out of a cannon into a brick wall just six feet away, would it be fatal? Well, I suppose it depends on whether or not you can die laughing. [As always, alter the name to suit your event/approach.]

My uncle fell into a vat of glue – and came to a sticky end.

My aunt was struck by lightning. That was a shock.

This place is so high class,   they give you a little bowl to wash your fingers in ... before you go to the loo.

This place is so high class ... there's a waiting list just to use the toilets.

That restaurant is so exclusive, they won't let you in unless you've already eaten.

The service in that restaurant is so slow, it's best to eat before you book a table.

Our local school is so over-subscribed, you have to put your child's name down before you've even met his mother.

Am I the only person who thinks collecting tea-cups is a mug's game?

I once killed two birds with one stone ... and got a severe reprimand from the RSPB.

The last time I saw a face that sad was when I told my wife I was leaving her for another woman. But it wouldn't be till after the weekend.

Never hit a man when he's down.   Especially if he's bigger than you.   He might get up again.

Scientists in America have crossed a shallot with a lap dancer … and can now grow an onion that peels itself.

Scientists at McDonald's have crossed David Beckham's DNA with a banana – and will shortly be marketing the world's thickest milkshake.

I read in the paper that a well-known Bishop is moving into the smallest house in Britain, with the randiest young actress in the country. He says he hopes it'll be a tight squeeze.

I read in the paper that the most accident-prone executioner in Iran was worried he was going to lose his job. Sadly, events overtook him, and he's just given himself the chop.

I read in the paper, an Iranian stand-up comic has applied for the job of state executioner.   It's all very humane. Apparently he gets prisoners to laugh their heads off.

Interesting piece in the paper yesterday about an asthmatic policeman. Apparently, he's always catching his own breath.

I saw a programme on the telly about a farmer in Kent who races herbs for fun. They say he's a man ahead of his thyme.

I saw in the paper the Pope has bowed to demands from mathematicians and given them their own saint.   A spokesman said, he was glad they'd no longer have to count their own blessings.

Darwin's theories – they've evolved over time.

I was a love child. When I was born, my dad took one look at me and said, 'For the love of God, what's that?'

The BBC were hoping to make a film about a man who steals furniture from people's homes, then renovates it. They invited him to the studio, but the moment he came through the door, he made a bolt for it.

I'm so lazy. I begin a sentence full of life and enthusiasm and then I can't even be bothered to…

The judge said, 'I'm going to give you a long sentence.' 'I don't mind,' said the prisoner, 'as long as you speak slowly.'

I'm worried about my mother-in-law's health. She seems to be getting better.

What's the last thing you should say to an MP? 'Take aim …. fire!'

Watching television broadens the mind.   And these days the stomach is often close behind.

I wouldn't say he's pale, but every time he lies down someone gives him the kiss of life.

Charities put out such boring adverts these days, I've completely lost the will to give.

I tried to become a traffic warden, but I failed the medical test. They found I had a heart.

I tried to join the police force. I took the intelligence test. Unfortunately, I passed, so they wouldn't let me in.

My wife's bark is worse than her bite. As long as she doesn't bite you.

A bird in the hand ... is worth seven yen in Tokyo.

I worked in holiday camps for a while. I had a spell as a magician.

I met my future wife at one of those wild, swingers parties where people throw off their clothes and jump on the first attractive stranger they fancy. I haven't told my present wife yet, it would only upset her.

Is a temporary grave-digger just filling in?

I once wrote a novel, and sent it off. It came back a week later with the following note: 'We have read between the lines and find as much interest there as elsewhere in your book.'

Britain has decided to send a man to the Moon. Nick Clegg [*or anyone else currently unpopular*].

In a bid to boost our track gold medal chances in the next Olympics, scientists have crossed the common cold with a cheetah, and come up with a nose that runs very fast.

I caught a cold last week. To be fair, it wasn't moving very fast.

Why is it the girls on the counter at McDonalds look as if they were in a pie-eating competition?   And they all won.

A man hit me on the head. That was a bit of a blow.

Someone once told me honesty was the best policy. But he was lying.

I wasn't driven to drink. I hailed a taxi.

I'm as fit as a flea.   Not a particularly well flea, it's true.

I went for a job. The hours were long, the pay poor and no pension. I said, 'I'd have to be a fool to work for you.' They said, 'Great, when can you start?'

My car is such a wreck, it's touch and go whether it expires before the tax disc.

My wife's a fine housekeeper. If I drop anything after she's tidied up, she fines me.

Behind every successful man … is the wife he's divorced in favour of a younger woman.

I hide my money in my gloves. I like to keep it handy.

Lawyers don't go to hell when they die. The devil's not that stupid.

Traffic wardens don't go to hell when they die. God is merciful – even to Satan.

He said, 'I play the piano by ear.' I said, 'Well, it was obvious you weren't using your hands.'

I could never keep a secret from my wife. Have you seen the size of her?

He pinched the nurse's bottom. But she made him put it back.

My wife and I met in Barnstaple. It was a marriage made in Devon.

Why do we say, 'He's the happiest man alive'? Who's the happiest man dead?

When I was young, I thought growing old was the worst thing that could happen to me. And do you know what – I was right.

My brother lights up every room he enters. He's an arsonist.

My sister's a bit of a goer. Last month she was seeing twins. Last week it was triplets and yesterday she went out with quads. She never dates single men.

I went into my local restaurant, and asked the waiter what he recommended. He said the place next door.

I was a Caesarean birth. My mother was very cut up about it.

I asked the flight attendant, 'When does the plane take off?' She said, 'Same time as always. When the wheels leave the ground.'

I can't stop thinking about shoes. It's my wife's fault. Yesterday she gave me a piece of her mind.

A man came up to me in the street. He said, 'Can you give me £10 for a cup of coffee?' I said, 'Why £10?' He said, 'I'd like a few biscuits with it.'

His mate said, 'Can you give me thirty quid for a cup of coffee?' I said, 'You're trying it on.' He said, 'No, just drinking it.'

I hear the government's decided to ban all left-handed activities. They say it's the right thing to do.

My girlfriend said, 'I go where my heart leads.' I said, 'I usually follow my legs.'

David Beckham went to see a mind reader. Before they began she said, 'That'll be fifteen quid.' He said, 'The sign on your door says it's only a fiver.' She said, 'Yes, but there's a ten pound search fee.'

A little old lady called a plumber in to fix a leak. He took one look at the tap and yelled, 'Out, out, out' several times, then said, 'That'll be fifty quid.' She said, 'Has that fixed it?' He said, 'No – that's just my "call out" charge.'

My mother-in-law has a razor sharp mind. If it dropped to her neck I'd be a happy man.

She has a memory like an elephant. And a body to match.

My brother's a professional footballer. Very competitive man. Can't bear to lose. He scored an own goal once – and immediately put in for a transfer to the other side.

On an MP's grave the headstone read, 'He is not dead, but only sleeping.' And underneath it someone had scrawled, 'Then for God's sake don't wake the bugger up.'

My wife said, 'Great minds think alike.' I said, 'I don't think they do.' She said, 'Proves my point, then.'

I don't like to take off my wedding ring. It upsets my wife. She think I'm going to leave her. And it's always a terrible blow when I don't.

I said to my wife, 'I've half a mind to argue the point.' She said, 'Well, when you find the other half, we'll get started.'

My brother is very successful. He has everything he wants. And I want everything he has.

Do you know, postmen are the only people who, when they're fired, they don't get the sack.

I'm not leaving anything when I go. I'm having all my money stamped, 'Not legal tender'.

I swallowed a watch this morning. Went to see the doctor. He gave me some tablets. I said, 'What will they do?' He said, 'They'll help you pass the time.'

I had a friend who overdosed on herbs. He went to see the doctor who gave him some tablets. He said, 'What are these for?' The doctor said, 'They'll help you pass the thyme.'

I couldn't remember where I'd left my boomerang – and then it came back to me.

I once met a fortune-telling gardener. He could look into the fuchsia.

Yesterday was a dark day for North Yorkshire [*or wherever you live*]. We had a power cut.

My wife enjoys lying on the beach. Mostly about her age.

Why do they call them speed bumps? There's no way you can speed over them.

Our education system is geared to achieving full employment for our nation's youth – at McDonalds.

Get your own back on the young. Put on Radio 2, full blast – then drive past a youth club with all your windows wound down.

When he left office, Tony Blair said the nation's future was safe in Gordon Brown's hands. Which was a bit like saying, Europe's future was safe with the French in 1939.

Tony Blair said he hopes New Labour's legacy is safe. Well, in the sense that no one knows where or what it is, it probably is.

Did you hear about the aggressive scuba diver? He went down fighting.

He said, 'Does Alzheimer's run in your family?' I said, 'I can't remember.'

He said, 'Does ignorance run in your family?' I said, 'I don't know.'

I'm getting quite for – for – for … it's no good, I can't remember.

My days are numbered. I'm not sick. I've just bought myself a calendar.

A lawyer is a man who says you're ruined because of something you did. You went to see him.

A friend is someone who has been to your house – and doesn't wipe his shoes on the way out.

He who laughs last … is just looking for attention.

I play soccer like Wayne Rooney. With a ball…

I'm not a well man. I fell down one once, it put me right off.

Man came up to me in the street. He said, 'My name's clapper.' I thought, 'That rings a bell.'

He said, 'My wife's name is Mary, she grew up a Catholic.' I said, 'Mine's is Ivy. She grew up a wall.'

I went to the travel agents. I said, 'Where can I go for fifty quid?' They said, 'The bank'd be a good start.'

So I went down the bank. I said, 'I've come about a loan.' They said, 'Thank God for that. How much can you lend us?'

I bought some bees last week. They came with a honey-back guarantee.

I once read a book on heavyweight boxing. I didn't understand it at first. Then it hit me.

My best friend is so mean, if he gives a waiter a tip, he gets no credit for it – because they don't believe it's him.

I met a young lady at a party last week. She asked me what I did for a living. I said, 'I'm a comic.' She said, 'Ooh – what? Like the Beano?'

I sold all my shares in Assassins Unlimited. Made a huge killing.

Gandalf arrived in Sydney this morning and immediately claimed political asylum. If it's granted, in future he'll be known as the Wizard of Oz.

My computer keeps freezing. It's my own fault, I shouldn't keep it in the fridge.

The sound man was so annoying, the director said to him, 'Do you want a kick up the boom?'

Marriage is for life. You only get time off for *bad* behaviour.

In Saudi Arabia, Ali stole a child's pram, for which the punishment was 20 years' imprisonment. With the police closing in, he jumped in a jeep and made his getaway. Back at his hideout, the other members of the gang said, 'You could have got another 30 years for stealing a jeep. Why'd you do it?' 'Well,' said Ali, 'I knew I couldn't survive 20 years in a Saudi jail, so I thought, "What the hell. I might as well be hanged for a jeep as a pram".'

I tell the kids, don't do needles. The only dope worth shooting is Nick Clegg [*or someone equally unpopular/stupid*].

Older people don't do drugs. It's not a moral thing – we can't work out the metric system.

How many policemen does it take to screw in a light bulb? No one knows – they haven't done the paperwork yet.

I knew someone once, spent a fortune on marijuana that was six months out of date. It was money for old dope.

A couple from Warsaw have filed for divorce after the husband moved to Britain in search of work. The wife said she suddenly realised that though they'd once been very close, they were now Poles apart.

I'd like to finish now – and you probably feel the same way – with a joke. An 8-foot Englishman, 9-foot Irishman and 10-foot Scotsman walk into a bar. I know what you're thinking – it's a tall story.

A LITTLE BIT NAUGHTY...

A few jokes, with a more 'adult' audience in mind…

A man came up to me in the street, he said, 'You're a magician make, my wife disappear.' I said, 'Everyone asks me to do that.' He said, 'Well, she's p****d a lot of people off.'

Did you hear about the blonde who seduced her philosophy teacher?   She blew his mind.

Acne is just Nature's way of reminding you not to kiss a teenager.

I found a rubber dildo in my cereal this morning. It was a new promotion – Porn Flakes.

What do you call a chocolate breakfast cereal that makes you impotent? Coco Flops.

My girlfriend's very health conscious. It's great when it comes to blow jobs, mind. I put on a fruit-flavoured condom and tell her it's one of her five a day.

My father gave me a dog for my birthday. Ugliest woman I've ever shagged, but boy could she go.

I was going to perform the chop cup naked. But I didn't have the balls.

Man walks into the doctor's surgery, blood streaming down his face, arm broken in three places, leg hanging off.   Doctor says, 'What happened to you?'   Man says, 'A midget hit me.' Doctor says, 'What was he – a master of unarmed combat?' 'No,' says the man, 'A f*****g truck driver.'

First time I met my wife, I said, 'I'd like to go to bed with you.' She said, 'You're very forward'. I said, 'No – just frightened of the dark.'

Saving for a rainy day? Have you seen interest rates? I'll be lucky if I can afford a f*****g umbrella!

You know it's time to go on a diet, when Dawn French points at you in the street and yells, 'Who's the skinny b*****d?'

I got my wife very excited in bed last night.   I said I was thinking of leaving her.

A man goes to his doctor and says, 'I feel like a woman.' 'When was the last time you had sex?' asks the doctor. 'Sod the sex,' says the man. 'It's three days since I bought a pair of shoes and it's driving me crazy.'

I wouldn't say David Beckham was cerebrally challenged … because the thick b*****d wouldn't know what I was talking about.

Scientists have crossed a violinist with a juggler and come up with a man who keeps fiddling with his balls.

I wanted to take my girlfriend up the aisle. But she said we'd have to wait till we were married.

My mum said I was a little b*****d when I was young. Well, she didn't know my father.

I once went out with a sex-mad arsonist. She shagged like a house on fire.

My first girlfriend was thrown out of the Army for being promiscuous. She couldn't keep her legs together long enough to stand to attention.

They say that not enough sex affects the mind. Personally, I think that's just crazy talk.

A man who's visited the same prostitute every day for the past 30 years has taken the week off in the hope it'll rekindle the old magic. Or in other words, he hopes 'Absence will make the tart grow fonder.'

'Going down?' asked the lift attendant. 'All right,' said the blonde, 'but it'll cost you a tenner.'

I like to see women in the nude. But every time I take my clothes off, someone calls the police.

Did you hear about the single teenage mother of four who won a leading role in a Shakespeare play? Asked what her favourite line was, she replied, 'If you f**k me, do I not breed?'

Did you hear about the newly married man who was so desperate to have sex with his wife he ran all the way home … and came through the front door?

Our vicar objects to sex before marriage. He says it puts the congregation off.

Prince Kee was very moral and strait-laced till he ascended to his father's throne. Then he became King Kee.

I dated a policewoman once. It didn't work out, though – she kept asking me to come quietly.

I snorted acid once. Never again. Burns your f*****g nose off.

What do you get when you take ecstasy and birth control pills? A trip without the kids.

When I young, I believed in puppy love. Of course, the puppy wasn't always so keen ….

ASSORTED PATTER

Just a few bits of patter, which you may find useful, inspirational, or even (and unintentionally on my part) familiar!

[*If someone laughs loudly*]

'Louder, sir [*or madam*] – and encourage all your friends. Tell them there's money in it.'

'I'd recognise that laugh anywhere. If only I knew who it was.'

[If people don't laugh when you want them to]

'If you don't find this act funny, I don't care – I'm just road-testing it for a friend. Of course, he's an ex-friend now.'

[To a heckler]

'Don't be shy, sir, tell us how you really feel.'

[To a heckler]

'You're too good for this show. I'd go home if I were you. Or possibly just into one.'

[To a heckler or aggressive – but smaller than you, just in case – audience member]

You look as though you've led a full life. I'm not sure what it is you're full of, but I'm standing downwind just in case.

[If you drop the cards – and who hasn't?]

'It was lucky the floor was there – they might have gone all the way down and hit an Aussie on the head.'

[If your mind goes blank]

'I can't remember what happens next. Would you mind applauding now and I'll do the trick later when it comes back to me?'

[When you have a problem with a sleight]

'This bit is complicated and takes years of practice, skill and training – for which, quite frankly, I don't have the time. So would you mind if I asked you all to look away for a few seconds?'

[*While shuffling Jumbo cards*]

'These aren't big cards, I just have very small hands.'

'This next trick has been banned in 23 European countries. Unfortunately for you, this isn't one of them.'

'This trick is best performed blindfolded, but if you don't have one just shut your eyes.'

'We haven't met beforehand, we've arranged nothing, is that right? ['Yes'] [*You move on*] 'It must have been someone else.' [*To another person*] 'Was it you I asked?' [*An old one, but a goodie, nonetheless!*]

'This trick has never been done before. With good reason. It's rubbish.'

'This trick has baffled the finest minds in Europe. And the French can't work it out either.' [*Replace with whoever you wish to annoy!*]

'I don't use sleight of hand. In fact, I do nothing with my hands at all. Everything I do, I do up here [*pointing to your head*]. My wife says, I can do a lot up here, because, quite frankly, there's a lot of room.'

'[IN A COMPETITION] Could someone lend me £20? It's not for a trick, I just thought it would be nice to take something home.'

[*While holding up two copies of the Daily Mirror*]

'This is a good trick. It's all done with Mirrors.'

'Many tricks are possible with a pack of cards. In the wrong company, you can make a lot of money disappear. Most of it your own.'

'I thought I'd begin with a trick I've never performed before. Then I thought, that's silly – I won't know how it's done.'

'I'm a comedy magician. Or as someone once said – my act is a joke.'

'My family laughed when I told them I wanted to be a comedy magician. They're not laughing now.' [*With grateful thanks to the late, great Bob Monkhouse.*]

BITS OF BUSINESS

A few odds and ends, ideas, bits of business etc which you may like to use, adapt or leave out for the dustmen…

'NO TEAR' TORN AND RESTORED NEWSPAPER

I was reading the paper earlier on. As you can see [*taking out first piece*] I was in a tearing hurry.

ON STAGE

Place a large photo of a naked (or scantily clad/attractive) woman on a stand on the far side of the stage from where you are working. Patter along the following lines, 'This is what we call misdirection. While you're watching her, you can't be watching me. And, quite frankly, if you are watching me instead of her, you're at the wrong show.'

Hand a sequinned bikini suit to a man you've just asked to assist you. Point to the side of the stage (or somewhere else out of sight), as you say, 'If you could just change into this round the back, sir, that would be marvellous. Thank you.'

[*Remove a large brick/knife from your briefcase and pretend to throw it into the audience*]

I will now choose a volunteer completely at random. Will whoever catches this… [*Another oldie, but one that always gets laughs!*]

MONEY MAGIC

I will now make this money disappear. Think of me as the Inland Revenue – only with feelings.

Do you have any spare change on you? That's spare? Then you don't need it? [*You pocket it*] Thank you. For my next trick… [*In doing so, you can, if necessary, swap any relevant cash for a gimmicked coin etc*]

Money. They say you can't take it with you. Well, why would you want to?

74

CARD MAGIC

[*Producing a pair of scissors*]

I shall now cut the deck. [*An old joke, surely – but it works!*]

[*Removing a large knife from your inside jacket/briefcase etc*]

I don't know what your card is, but I think I'll take a wild stab.

MINDREADING MAGIC

[*Before a book test*] Please call out any number between one and 400. [*When the number is called out, look at the page – or pretend to. Then hand the book over, looking as cheeky as possible and ask your helper to turn to that page.*] Please look at the first word on that page …

ROPE MAGIC

[*Producing ropes*]

I paid five quid for these. Second hand. Money for old rope.

Three pieces of rope, all different sizes. You're thinking to yourself, he's going to do that trick where he makes them all the same length. [*Take out scissors and cut into similar lengths*] You're right.

And that's it! There's no more. I hope you've had fun. If you have, head off out now and have some more!

BIBLIOGRAPHY

Below is a selection of books that I have in my own library, and which I would heartily recommend to the budding comedy writer and/or stand-up performer.

Ashton, Brad, *How To Write Comedy,* Elm Tree Books, 1983

Ashton, Brad, *The Job of a Laughtime*, Lulu.com, 2011

Carter, Judy, *The Comedy Bible,* Fireside, 2001

Fechtner, Leopold, *5000 One- and Two-line Jokes*, Thorsons, 1979

Helitzer, Melvin, *Comedy Writing Secrets,* Writer's Digest Books, 1987

Holloway, Sally, *The Serious Guide to Joke Writing*, BookShaker, 2010

Keable, Ian, *Stand-Up: A Professional Guide to Comedy Magic*, 2008

Kirkpatrick, Betty (Ed), *Chambers Dictionary of Idioms and Catchphrases,* Chambers, 1995

Metcalf, Fred (Ed), *The Penguin Dictionary of Humorous Quotations,* Penguin Books, 1986

Metcalf, Fred (Ed), *The Penguin Dictionary of Jokes,* Penguin Books, 1993

Monkhouse, Bob, *Just Say a Few Words*, Lennard Publishing, 1988

Murray, Logan, *Be a Great Stand-Up,* Teach Yourself, 2010

Perret, Gene, *Comedy Writing Step by Step*, Samuel French Trade, 1982

Perret, Gene, *Shift Your Writing Career into High Gear,* Writer's Digest Books, 1993

Perret, Gene, *Successful Stand-Up Comedy,* Samuel French, 1993

Perret, Gene, *Comedy Writing Workbook*, Players Press Inc, 1994

Rees, Nigel, *The Guinness Dictionary of Jokes*, Guinness Publishing, 1995

Roche, Jenny, *Get Your Act Together,* Compass Books, 2014

Vorhaus, John, *The Comix Toolbox*, Silman-James Press, 1994